England in colour

Introduction and commentaries by J. H. B. Peel

B. T. BATSFORD LTD LONDON

We hope this bring back
some happy memories

Betty & Ken..

Dec. 1969.

First published 1969

© B. T. Batsford Ltd 1969

Made and printed in Denmark by F. E. Bording Ltd, Copenhagen
for the publishers B. T. Batsford Ltd, 4 Fitzhardinge Street, London W1

7134 0017 X

Contents

Introduction

Like Rome itself, the English scene was not built in one day. It originated as part of what is now the Continent of Europe, from which it was severed by an upheaval that begat the English Channel and the North Sea. Thereafter an island of forest and moor was felled, tilled, and made fertile by generations of settlers. Green tracks appeared, and then metal roads, linking the scattered communities. Cave-dwellings crumbled and were replaced by cottages, castles, cathedrals. Hedges and stone walls created the patterns of private enterprise. So, down the centuries, each generation wrought change; and we cannot understand the look of the land until we have made the acquaintance of its people.

Who *are* the English? They are the descendants of Celts, Romans, Saxons, Jutes, Angles, Vikings, Normans; that being more or less the sequence of invaders who left their indelible mark upon the roads, fields, buildings, dialects, and place-names of England. Why were these hybrid people called English? The answer to that question is complex because the word 'England' is a corruption of *Engle-land*, the land of the *Engle* or Angles. Why then did these *Engle* give their name to their new home? Nobody knows. The *Engle* themselves came from Slesvig in Germany. They were neither more numerous nor more gifted than any other of the permanent settlers. And yet, for reasons unknown to us, the land was named after them. As early as the year 897 the word *Englisc* was used both of the people and of their language. Mourning the decay of scholarship in a country harried by warfare, King Alfred reported that few men south of Lincolnshire could translate a Latin letter into English *(of Laedene on Englisc)*.

Even today an Englishman is surprised—and overseas visitors bewildered—by the variety of English dialects; but in Chaucer's time a Kentish man would have sounded almost unintelligible to a Cumbrian, and each would have failed to understand a Devonian. Nor was this

Babel based solely on differences in pronunciation; many of the commonest words varied with the regions. Cornwall, indeed, spoke its own Celtic language, and continued to speak it until the eighteenth century.

Both Scotland and Wales had their regionalism, but it was simple and clear-cut, being between the north and the south of those two countries. Moreover the regionalism was curbed by the need to unite against England. The English, by contrast, had no such permanent stimulus, at any rate after the Norman conquest. In view therefore of the variety of their language and landscape, it is remarkable that they ever did achieve the unity which Shakespeare found:

> *This happy breed of men, this little world . . .*
> *This blessed plot, this earth, this realm, this England.*

England became—and to some extent remains—a unity of regions; or, more precisely, of countries. A Cumbrian, for example, will tell you: 'There's nobut two counties in England, and the second is Westmorland.' It was said of certain English regiments that they regarded the last war as a battle between Yorkshire and the Rest. Certainly each county wears its own look. Lower Slaughter, a Gloucestershire village of pasture and stone, cannot be mistaken for Chaddesley Corbett, a Worcestershire village of orchards and timber. Even a single county contains its regionalism. Thus the brick-and-flint cottages of the Buckinghamshire Chilterns differ conspicuously from the timbered houses along the border with Northamptonshire. Again, Bodmin Moor in east Cornwall seems altogether another land when compared with the sylvan softness of Helford River in south Cornwall. Up north, a man from Keswick detects a difference in the dialect of the man from Coniston Water; yet Keswick and Coniston are both in Lakeland. Such is the legacy of geology and genealogy.

But a *caveat* must be entered, for many of these endearing differences, once the essence of Englishry, are dwindling and seem likely to die. Even today there are villagers within forty miles of London who have never visited either the coast or the capital; but their grandchildren take summer holidays in Majorca, and speak with the broadcast patois of

Hollywood and London. A sociologist, Dr Mark Abrams, forecast that by the year 1983 England will contain no large tract of uninhabited countryside: 'Britain', he declared, 'may well become the first model of a predominantly suburbanised community.'

And yet one wonders. In the Yorkshire dales and on the Westmorland fells it is possible to walk all day without sighting anything larger than a farmhouse; in the far west, Exmoor holds its ancient fastness; and although Lakeland has become a summer car queue, its wintry lanes are lonely and therefore at ease in their natural state. Moreover, large tracts of rural England either belong to the National Trust or are included within the National Parks. There seems no valid reason to suppose that those areas will soon find themselves defenceless against so-called economic necessity. Man shall not live by exports alone. The land still sustains the outward and visible signs of his inward and spiritual grace. Walter de la Mare spoke for every countryman who draws strength from the hills and woods of home:

> *Thine be the woods whereto my soul,*
> *Out of the noontide beam,*
> *Flees for a refuge green and cool*
> *And tranquil as a dream.*

Instead, therefore, of guessing what England may resemble in the future, let us know what she looks like at present; beginning with a definition of the principal regions, as follows: London, the South, the West, the Midlands, the East, the North.

LONDON

From time immemorial London has been the hub of English history. Here came most of the invaders, not least among them the heralds of Christianity. Here were the trade routes to the Continent; and here the river that led from those routes into the heart of the capital. Other cities have their riches, but none can vie with the number and splendour of the famous buildings in and around London: the Tower, Windsor Castle, Buckingham Palace, Hampton Court, St Paul's Cathedral, Syon House. Daniel Defoe was justified when he described London as

'. . . opulent, enlarged, and still increasing.' It continues to increase. Greater London contains upward of eight million people, and extends nearly twenty miles from Marble Arch. Although it has indeed become shapeless and overpopulated, London remains a vast harbour, a financial clearing house, a centre of the arts, the seat of government.

THE SOUTH

The South may be defined as the whole, or parts of, the counties of Berkshire, Hampshire, Kent, Middlesex, Surrey, Sussex.

This region, the seed-bed of English culture, is the gentlest of all landscapes; sometimes relatively high, as on the Sussex Downs; sometimes comparatively lonely, as on the Romney Marshes. And everywhere the variety reveals itself. You find stone and timbered houses at Alfriston in Sussex; thatched cottages at Chilbolton in Hampshire; redbrick mansions on the Berkshire Downs (a notable cantering ground for race horses). Here are the cathedrals of Canterbury, Chichester, Salisbury; here the great abbey of Romsey; all etching a skyline that was set to music by Robert Bridges:

Now blessed be the towers
that crown England so fair,
That stand up in prayer
unto God for our souls.

Men laboured through many centuries to lay the foundation of these trim fields and noble buildings, for much of Sussex and Kent was covered by a weald or forest. Old William Camden reported a tradition that this weald '. . . was a great while together in manner nothing else than a desert and waste wilderness, not planted with towns or people, as the outsides of the shire were, but stored and stuffed with herds of deer and droves of hogs only'. That ancient forest is now a densely-populated suburb of London. People travel fifty miles from Brighton to their work in Cobbett's 'great Wen'. The local dialects, too, are less varied than in the North, West, and Midlands. Even so, the South of England contains many oases of unspoiled villages and country towns: Poynings, Brede Lewes, Tenterden, Sutton Valence, Glynde. And again the motif is variety . . . the creeks at Bosham and the Hamble River where summer yachtsmen ply their craft . . . the pine-clad heaths of Surrey . . . the 'sweet Thames' which Edmund Spenser praised, flowing from Teddington to its source in a Cotswold meadow near Cirencester.

Above all, the South is a land of sunlight. From Margate to Bournemouth the rival holiday resorts announce themselves as sun-drenched and drier than the North and West. This was the country of Rudyard Kipling, of Edward Thomas, and of Hilaire Belloc who spoke for the South when he said:

> *Here am I homeward from my wandering,*
> *Here am I homeward and my heart is healed.*

THE WEST

The West may be defined as the counties of Cornwall, Dorset, Devonshire, Somerset, Wiltshire.

G. M. Trevelyan believed that 'The places where fairies might still dwell lie for the most part west of the Avon.' Certainly the West is the most magical corner of England, no matter how you choose to define wizardry. Stonehenge, whose boulders were dragged and perhaps floated from Wales, remains Europe's outstanding memorial of prehistory. From Cornwall to Somerset, King Arthur and his Court littered the land with legends (and archaeologists seem likely to dig up some facts about them). The further West you go, the softer everything becomes, not in a silly but in the sinewy sense. The winter sun is warm; frost scarcely touches some of the south Devon combes. Dialect, too, loses its harshness. You might mistake the Stafford accent for Nottingham's, but no man who knows England will suppose that a Cornish fisherman speaks like a Durham collier.

Cornwall is a law unto itself, though repealed each summer by the holiday hordes. Its place-names alone compose a poem: Advent, St Anthony-in-Roseland, Come-to-Good, Mawgan-in-Meneage, Zennor, Zone, Ruan Lanihorne, Perranzabuloe, Amalabrea, Chyandor. There are so many Cornish saints that Heaven scarcely contains room for any man born north of the Tamar. The green fields at Trelissick, the blue waters of Helford River, the heather on Bodmin Moor; that is Cornwall in all its colours.

Devon and Somerset follow the same pattern writ larger. To the author of *Lorna Doone* Devonshire seemed '. . . the fairest county in England'. Thomas Hardy preferred his native Dorset, which he re-created as the hero of his best novels. Wiltshire's wheatfields and ancient monuments were the home of Richard Jefferies and Maurice Hewlett. There are many famous buildings in the West: Wells Cathedral, Bath Abbey, Corfe Castle, Sherborne School, Montacute House. Some of the villages are household names: Dunster, Lacock, Castle Combe. But the loveliest things lie off the beaten track . . . Aisholt in the Quantocks, home of Sir Henry Newbolt who wrote *Drake's Drum* . . . the lane from Sicily Cottage to Great Bedwyn in Wiltshire's Savernake Forest . . . the riverside path from Hunters Inn to the Severn Sea in Devon . . . the waterscape at Horner Woods and a dizzy lane therefrom to Stoke Pero, the highest church on Exmoor . . . the No Through Road from Gerrans to Percuil, which walks the plank of a Cornish creek and then dives into the water. Above all, the West is the cradle of our English seamanship, from Bideford to Brixham, from Appledore to Plymouth. Drake, Raleigh, Hawkins, Frobisher; each in his day uttered John Masefield's imperative:

> *I must go down to the seas again,*
> *To the lonely sea and the sky,*
> *And all I ask is a tall ship*
> *And a star to steer her by.*

THE MIDLANDS

The Midlands may be defined as the whole, or parts of, Buckinghamshire, Gloucestershire, Herefordshire, Leicestershire, Monmouthshire, Northamptonshire, Nottinghamshire, Oxfordshire, Rutland, Shropshire, Staffordshire, Warwickshire, Worcestershire.

This is the most mixed of all the regions, for it includes the industrial ugliness of Birmingham and the Black Country, the quietude of Shrop-

shire's border with Wales, the fox-hunting Shires, the wooded banks
of the Severn, the Chiltern Hills, the mountainous seclusion of Monmouthshire, the pastures and hopfields of Herefordshire. The architecture is as varied as the landscape. At Fotheringhay in Northamptonshire
the stone houses resemble those at Chipping Campden in Gloucestershire. Shropshire and Herefordshire, on the other hand, are famed for
their magpie or black-and-white houses, so-called because the oak
timbers shine like ebony on a whitewashed background. Among industrial areas many of the houses are of brick. Different, too, is the accent.
In Gloucestershire, on the edge of the West Country, you overhear an
echo from Wiltshire; in Monmouthshire (basically a Welsh county) the
lilt is audibly un-English. This, the centre of England, sang its own
lullaby to John Drinkwater:

> *I turn to sleep, content that from my sires*
> *I draw the blood of England's midmost shires.*

Despite some industrial zones, the Midlands contain country as deep
as any in the southern half of England: the green lanes of Warwickshire
that wander from Honington to Idlicote (Shakespeare himself may have
followed them) . . . the Chiltern Hills above Ipsden, and the track to
Drunken Bottom . . . the grassy Watling Street near Church Stretton . . .
the hair-pin lane (formerly a coaching road) over the hills from Lingen
to Wales . . . the Malvern Hills in Worcestershire (Celia Fiennes
called them 'The English Alps').

When Daniel Defoe toured England two centuries ago he noted three
Midland highways, 'the Icknild Way, the Watling-street, and the Foss'.
The Icknield Way was a Celtic grassway between East Anglia and the
West; the Watling Street was a Roman road; the Fosse Way, another
Roman road, led from Lincoln to Devonshire (parts of the original
paving can still be seen). Like Durham, the cathedral at Worcester is
set above a river; the tower of Gloucester cathedral transcends an
industrial city; Buildwas Abbey, beside the Severn, is comparable with
Tintern Abbey on the Wye; the spires of Oxford still dream above the
industrial desecration. The fairest part of the Midlands—the western
sector—retains a mysteriousness which Mary Webb distilled:

A lone green valley, good for sheep,
Where still the ancient fairies keep
Their right of way and copyhold
All night with mullein torches.

THE EAST

East Anglia may be defined as the whole, or parts of, Bedfordshire, Cambridgeshire, Essex, Hertfordshire, Huntingdonshire, Norfolk, Suffolk.

Throughout the middle ages East Anglia was the wealthiest corner of the kingdom, growing rich on wheat and wool. From Ipswich to King's Lynn its ports carried most of the nation's overseas trade. Then came the industrial revolution which put England's eggs into one basket. Cheaply imported food robbed East Anglia of a market, and the region became a backwater, still agricultural, but no longer a great influence in affairs. Today the peacefulness has been disturbed by the growth of Ipswich as a factory zone. King's Lynn, too, may change from a country town to an industrial estate. At present, however, East Anglia is deeply rural despite its nearness to London.

Led by Norwich Cathedral, the churches are monuments to the pious prosperity of the merchants who built them. Suffolk was the home of a miller's son, John Constable, who said of East Bergholt: 'I love even every stile and stump, and every lane in the village.' His famous Mill at Flatford belongs to the National Trust, and is a centre for naturalists.

Again the architecture varies. Norfolk, for example, has the brick-and-flint work that is found in the Chilterns also. Many Suffolk farms are thatched and timbered. Lavenham is perhaps the most beautiful country town in Britain, a maze of mediaeval houses and a spacious church. The coast is cold, dry, flat; fascinating to all who love birds and the North Sea coasters. Felixstowe is a popular holiday resort; Aldeburgh is the home of a composer, Benjamin Britten, and the birthplace of a poet, George Crabbe, who set the scene of eighteenth-century amphibious activity:

Yon is our quay! those smaller hoys from town,
Its various wares, for country-use, bring down;
Those laden waggons, in return, impart
The country-produce to the city mart . . .

A coast road plays hide-and-seek between sand dunes and fertile farmland. Here Vice-Admiral Viscount Nelson, Duke of Bronte, was born—son of the rector of Burnham Thorpe. Here, at Holkham Hall, Thomas Coke, Earl of Leicester, added a new and scientific look to English farming. Fame, in fact, hangs like a necklace from this small region: Oliver Cromwell was a Huntingdonshire squire, Newmarket became the Mecca of horse-racing, Cambridge is a university famous throughout the world. Defoe disliked the Fens (''tis a horrid air for a stranger to breath'), but he admired the rich acres and the Norfolk Broads with their '. . . infinite number of wild fowl, such as duck and mallard, teal and widegeon, brand geese, wild geese . . .'. And Charles Kingsley, a Devonian, praised the Fens' astringent charm: 'They have a beauty of their own . . . A beauty as of the sea, of boundless expanse and freedom.'

THE NORTH

The North may be defined as the counties of Cheshire, Cumberland, Derbyshire, Durham, Lancashire, Lincolnshire, Northumberland, Westmorland, Yorkshire.

This region begins at the Peak District of Derbyshire, a land so steep and wild that Bishop Fuller declared: 'God, who is truly thaumaturgus, the only worker of wonders, hath more manifested his might in this than in any other county of England.' Here, amid a pattern of drystone walls, you meet the voice of the North. You also feel its temperature, for, as Gilbert White observed: 'The effects of heat are seldom very remarkable in the northern climate of England.'

Cheshire, a grazing county, is noted for its diary produce. Three centuries ago Celia Fiennes commented on the farmers' '. . . great Cheeses'. Yorkshire's three Ridings cover nearly four million acres. The West Riding alone could swallow England's second largest county,

Lincolnshire. Yorkshire overlooks both the Midlands and the Scottish Lowlands. Despite its industrial zones, the county is a vast farm with many moors and mountains.

Lancashire, the cotton-spinning county, includes Coniston Water and some of the grandest scenery in Lakeland. The Lancashire village of Hale was chosen by Thomas Carlyle's wife as '. . . the beautifullest village in all England'.

Durham is dour, industrial; yet it, too, has wide moors. Westmorland and Cumberland are the counties of lakes and mountains; overflowing in summer, but at other mid-week seasons aloof and majestic. Between Kendal and Keswick you have the most dramatic landscape in England. Cumberland is marred by some industrial zones along the coast, but around Appleby and Kirkby Lonsdale in Westmorland the lanes go their own way and are restful.

Northumberland—the land beyond the Humber—reaches so far north that it looks back on the Scottish hills. G. M. Trevelyan called it '. . . the land of far horizons'. These high and wind-winced solitudes were once a no-man's-land in the Border warfare; whence the peel towers or fortified houses, as at Elsdon.

This cold north country and its cordial people have sired many famous artists. Tennyson was born at Somersby Rectory on the Lincolnshire Wolds; Swinburne came from Capheaton Hall in Northumberland (and Capability Brown was born at Kirkharle nearby). Like Mrs Gaskell, the Brontë sisters lived for the north; Delius, that exotic plant, came from Bradford; and who has not heard of Grace Darling of Bamburgh in Northumberland? Brusque, stubborn, kindly; the people resemble their landscape. And the greatest of them all, William Wordsworth, discovered that the mountains are associated:

> *Not with the mean and vulgar works of man,*
> *But with high objects, with enduring things,*
> *With life and nature.*

THE THAMES AND THE HOUSES OF PARLIAMENT

'The Thames', said John Burns, 'is liquid history.' From the estuary to its source in a Cotswold meadow near Cirencester, the river has witnessed most of the major crises in the life of England. The Tower, St Paul's, Westminster Abbey, Whitehall, Hampton Court, Windsor Castle, the University of Oxford . . . all stand within a stone's throw of the Thames.

Big Ben—seen here in the middle distance—began to chime in 1859. It owes its name to Sir Benjamin Hall, who was then Commissioner of Works. This famous clock has never varied more than four seconds from Greenwich Time; only twice has it failed (once, in 1944, during an air raid). The river is still a highway for commerce. In 1968 some thirteen million tons of coal were carried by water, and the Port of London had five thousand barges or lighters.

WESTMINSTER

When the Palace of Westminster—that is, the Houses of Parliament—was burned down in 1834, many Londoners suggested that it should be rebuilt in Green Park, but the Duke of Wellington wisely insisted that Parliament ought not to be placed in a position so easily surrounded by the mob. The new Palace was therefore rebuilt on the site of the old, to a design by Charles Barry. Work began in 1840, and ended in 1867. Some people mock the architecture, but Dr Pevsner is not among them; he described the Palace as 'The most imaginatively planned and the most excellently executed major secular building of the Gothic revival anywhere in the world.'

Of the ancient Palace of Westminster, only the Great Hall remains; William Rufus built it in 1097; Richard II rebuilt it in 1398. Members of the Lower House bow to the Speaker's Chair because their predecessors met in the Palace Chapel of St. Stephen, where they bowed to the altar.

THE NATIONAL GALLERY and ST MARTIN-IN-THE-FIELDS

The National Gallery contains Britain's most important collection of paintings. It was built (1832-8) to a design by Wilkins; and enlarged several times between 1876 and 1961. The genesis of the gallery was a collection of 38 Angerstein pictures, purchased in 1824, at a cost of £57,000. Among the paintings were Hogarth's *Marriage à-la-Mode* and Titian's *Venus and Adonis*. In 1918 a State grant enabled the National Gallery to acquire many nineteenth-century works by foreign artists. During the last war Dame Myra Hess gave piano recitals in the gallery.

Seen in the background, the church of St Martin-in-the-Fields has become a household name, largely because many of its services were broadcast during the early years of radio. Its social workers offer an especial welcome to all who 'travail and are heavy laden'.

TRAFALGAR SQUARE

At dawn on 21st October, 1805, Vice-Admiral Viscount Nelson, Duke of Bronte, appeared on the quarter-deck of his flagship, *HMS Victory*, cruising off Cape Trafalgar. Gazing eastward, he sighted Bonaparte's fleet. At noon, as the enemy drew within range, Nelson made his immortal signal: 'England expects that every man will do his duty.' A few hours later, having saved Europe from lasting captivity, he died of his wounds.

Twelve years later a tardy nation began to clear a site for Nelson's monument, opposite the church of St Martin-in-the-Fields; but it was not until the reign of Queen Victoria that the monument was finished. Today the heirs of Nelson feed the pigeons, or harangue the crowd, while 'the saviour of Europe' thinks his thoughts,

> *. . . riding the sky*
> *With one arm and one eye.*

CHRISTMAS IN TRAFALGAR SQUARE

Piccadilly attracts the revellers, but Trafalgar Square evokes a deeper and more lasting joy; for a national hero baptised the place with his lifeblood, and a famous church stands by, waiting to receive any who will enter, regardless of age or colour or class or creed. Every Christmas a Norwegian tree sparkles in frostlight, or as a beacon through fog.

Sometimes the Christmas service is broadcast from St Martin-in-the-Fields, and then it reaches even to the mountains of England, so that the message is received by countless countryfolk, as Robert Bridges received it long ago:

> *The old words came to me*
> *By the riches of time*
> *Mellowed and transfigured*
> *As I stood on the hill*
> *Hearkening in the aspect*
> *Of the eternal silence.*

THE QUEEN VICTORIA MEMORIAL

At five o'clock on the morning of 20th June, 1837, the Archbishop of Canterbury and the Lord Chamberlain arrived at Kensington Palace, having galloped from Windsor Castle with dramatic news. A young girl received them, still in a dressing-gown. Seeing her, the two men fell upon their knees. That was how Victoria of England learned that she had become Queen. Sixty-four years later she died, having won the English people as no other Sovereign ever had won them since the first Queen Elizabeth.

The Queen's memorial was well-placed, facing the Palace which she made into a royal home. The Victorian era begat Tennyson, Lister, Dickens, Darwin, Emily Brontë, Brunel, Elgar, Winston Churchill, and Francis Thompson, who spoke for them all when he wrote:

They passed, they passed, but cannot pass away,
For England feels them in her blood like wine.

BUCKINGHAM PALACE

In 1703 the Duke of Buckingham and Normanby built a mansion which George III purchased in 1762. George IV employed John Nash to build a new mansion on the site, called Buckingham Palace. When the King died, in 1830, the rebuilding was still unfinished; so, Nash gave way to Edward Blore, who completed the task, covered much of Nash's work with a façade, and removed his Marble Arch. William IV disliked the new Palace—he preferred Windsor Castle—and it was not until Victoria ascended the throne that Buckingham Palace became the chief residence of the Royal Family. In 1913 a new façade was added by Sir Aston Webb. The grounds west and south-west of the Palace cover some forty-three acres (and are overlooked by a horribly high block of offices).

Buckingham Palace acts like a magnet. In time of peace it attracts visitors from all parts of the world; during a crisis it draws together the English people, who love the Monarch as a person, and revere the Monarchy as an institution, aloof from politics.

THE ROYAL HORSE GUARDS

The person of the Sovereign and the safety of the capital were long ago entrusted to two regiments of cavalry and five of infantry. The infantry comprises the Grenadier, Coldstream, Scots, Irish and Welsh Guards; the cavalry regiments are the Life Guards and the Royal Horse Guards, sometimes called the Household Troops.

Raised in 1661, and known as 'The Blues' because of their blue tunics, the Horse Guards fought at Sedgemoor, at the Boyne, and at Dettingen (where George II became the last King of England to lead his troops into battle). In 1812 the regiment served in Spain under Wellesley. They were present at the relief of Mafeking, and in France and Flanders throughout the 1914 War. During the Second World War they served overseas as mechanised infantrymen. Their ceremonial duties now add twopennorth of colour to a plainly penny world. The Colonel-in-Chief of the Royal Horse Guards is Her Majesty Queen Elizabeth II.

GROSVENOR SQUARE

Grosvenor Square today is a busy place, flanked by offices and embassies and showrooms. But elderly people remember the Square when it was quiet and wholly residential, the home of Society during the London season. The Square itself is named after the landowners, the Grosvenors, who were created Dukes of Westminster in 1874.

Although their dukedom is recent, the family is ancient. The first duke, Hugh Lupus Grosvenor, bore the name of his Norman ancestor, Hugh Lupus (the Wolf), first Earl of Chester. The Grosvenors received an earldom during the eighteenth century, and a marquisate in 1831. Their London residence, Grosvenor House, has been demolished; their ancestral seat is Eaton Hall at Eccleston in Cheshire. The family fortune was founded in 1676 when Sir Thomas Grosvenor married Mary Davies, the eleven-year-old heiress to the Ebury estates at Pimlico and Belgrave Square.

CHELSEA PENSIONERS

The Chelsea Royal Hospital was founded, at the suggestion of Charles II, by Sir Stephen Fox, to be a haven for five hundred retired or invalided soldiers. Later, a system of out-pensioning helped many veterans throughout the British Empire.

Standing in extensive grounds, which include the old Ranelagh Gardens, the Royal Hospital was built (1682-92) by Sir Christopher Wren. Its brickwork—with stone quoins, cornices, and window dressings—reveal Wren's genius for achieving an impressive effect with simple materials. The pensioners themselves are proud to wear the uniform of a bygone age, and the medals of famous campaigns. They receive a special cheer when they march with their heirs at the British Legion's annual Festival of Remembrance for those who died during two world wars. Here, in the words of Coleridge,

An old, deserving soldier makes his way.

THE TATE GALLERY

Henry Tate was born in 1819, at Chorley, which in those years was a small country town, some twenty-five miles north of Manchester. He became a wealthy sugar merchant, able to indulge his flair for the fine arts and to collect many valuable pictures. Shortly before he died, in 1899, he received a baronetcy, having founded the gallery which bears his name.

The Tate Gallery was opened in 1897. Its formal name is The National Gallery of British Art, and it is controlled by the Trustees of the National Gallery. Many famous British pictures are hung here, including works by Constable, Gainsborough, and Whistler. There is a special Turner wing, built by Sir Joseph Duveen and his son, Lord Duveen (1910); the latter subscribed towards the cost of housing works by foreign artists, and also to a sculpture hall (1937).

THE OLD CURIOSITY SHOP

'Night is generally my time for walking.' That is the opening sentence of Dickens's *Old Curiosity Shop*. It is also a description of his own compulsive temperament. During one of those City walks, Dickens found the bric-à-brac shop which appears in his story of Little Nell. The shop, he said, '. . . was one of those receptacles for old and curious things which seem to crouch in odd corners of the town . . .'.

But the shop and Little Nell are not the only vivid characters in this novel. Dickens triumphed by the force of genius. We forgive the over-writing, but we cannot forget the superabundance of creativity. Do you remember the Marchioness, that faithful servant (Dickens had met her in a debtors' prison)? Do you remember Mr Quilp, Dick Swiveller, Sampson Brass? All have outlived fashion, for all were created whitehot on the anvil of the richest imagination in English fiction.

ST JAMES'S PARK

This royal park covers ninety-three acres, and extends from Buckingham Palace to Whitehall. The suspension bridge was built in 1957, to replace a bridge of 1857. The ornamental lake covers twelve acres. St James's Park, which used to be a fashionable sauntering ground, is nowadays peopled by lunchtime office workers and by many others who find themselves 'in city pent'. Its graceful trees and greensward form a memorable hub, leading down the Mall towards Whitehall and the Admiralty Arch, and to Birdcage Walk, the headquarters of the Brigade of Guards at Wellington Barracks. The office of Master Gunner of St James's Park is held by a General.

St James's Palace, built by Henry VIII, was a royal residence from 1697 until 1837. Foreign ambassadors and ministers are still accredited to the Court of St James. In 1953 the Royal Chapel was opened for public worship at certain times of the year.

ST PAUL'S CATHEDRAL

'If you seek my monument, look around you.' So said Sir Christopher Wren to all who entered this cathedral. Wren's noble concept was thirty-five years in the making, from 1675 until 1710. The cost was £747,660; today it would be nearer £20,000,000. The inner cupola stands 218 feet above the floor; the Cross on the dome, 365 feet above the street. The Great Paul Bell in the south-west tower weighs 17 tons. Grinling Gibbons carved the choir stalls and also the organ casing. The famous Whispering Gallery has remarkable acoustic qualities.

In 1958 the choir and the high altar were restored, having been damaged during the blitz. The north transept was restored in 1962. The Chapel of the Most Excellent Order of the British Empire, in the crypt, was dedicated in 1960. Among the Deans of St Paul's were John Donne and William Ralph Inge.

TOWER BRIDGE

Eight years in the making, Tower Bridge was opened in 1894. Its Gothic turrets stand two hundred feet apart, linked to either bank by a suspension bridge. Between them, the bridge itself can be raised, in two parts, to allow large vessels to pass underneath. The names on the sterns of those ships box the compass: Bremen, Las Palmas, Leningrad, Toronto. High above, the architect built a bridge for pedestrians. Nearby stands the Tower of London, which gave its name to the bridge.

During the last war the little ships of the Royal Naval Auxiliary Patrol passed under Tower Bridge many times each day and night, standing watch over the Pool and the Port. England's sailor-poet, John Masefield, painted this riverscape:

> *The great street paved with water, filled with shipping,*
> *And all the world's flags flying, and the seagulls dipping.*

THE TOWER OF LONDON

'Who goes there?'

'The keys.'

'Whose keys?'

'The Queen's keys.'

Each night a guard goes the rounds, lit by a lantern, to the jingle of a Warder's keys. A bearskinned officer presents his sword, the Last Post pierces the darkness, another day is done.

Our great-grandchildren should live to celebrate the Tower's thousandth birthday. Through Traitor's Gate, the door to death, passed Sir Thomas More, Archbishop Cranmer, Queens Anne Boleyn and Catherine Howard, Sir Walter Raleigh. Until Stuart times the Tower was a palace; it still is a barracks, built to defend and to overawe the City (though it lies without the bounds). Here, more surely than in any other secular building, Time marches on, to an ancient tune.

'Who goes there?'

'The keys.'

GREENWICH

'One of the most sublime sights English architecture affords' . . . so said Sir Charles Reilly of the Royal Naval College beside the Thames at Greenwich. An earlier palace on the site was built by Humphrey, son of Henry IV. Henry VIII was born there, and there Edward VI died. In 1664 Charles II began to build a new palace, but ran short of money when only one block had been finished. In 1694, to mark the victory of the English Fleet at La Hogue, Queen Mary gave the building as a naval equivalent of the Royal Chelsea Hospital for soldiers.

Designed by Wren, the Royal Naval Hospital fulfilled its role until 1869. Four years later it became the Royal Naval College for the further training of naval officers. The Painted Hall—the Royal Navy's most colourful shrine—is sometimes used for State occasions. The President of the College is by custom a Rear-Admiral.

SYON HOUSE

Syon House stands near the River Thames at Brentford in Middlesex. In 1431 Henry VI, a pious man, granted permission for a Nunnery of Syon to be built here. A century later, when religious houses were dissolved, the building and lands reverted to the Crown. In 1578 they were granted to the ninth Earl of Northumberland. In 1632 Inigo Jones was commissioned to repair the building; in 1766 Robert Adam completely re-decorated the interior, and added the entrance gateway.

The Earls—and afterwards the Dukes—of Northumberland used the House as their town residence. They also owned Northumberland House, a mansion in the Strand, from which, in 1874, was brought the device of a lion which now stands on the river front. Syon House remains the London seat of the Duke of Northumberland, and is open to the public at certain times between April and September.

HAMPTON COURT PALACE

When Cardinal Wolsey was at the zenith of his power, he outshone even the King's retinue. Although he already owned magnificent houses at More in Shropshire and at Tittenhanger in Hertfordshire, he built himself this palace by the Thames. The poet Skelton stated the Cardinal's eminence:

> *Why come ye not to court?*
> *To whyche court?*
> *To the Kynge's Court,*
> *Or to Hampton Court?*

Wolsey spent only a short time here, for in 1520 he presented the palace to the King. During his residence, the Cardinal's retinue consumed two thousand sheep in one year, and more than four hundred oxen. Wren was employed to demolish and then rebuild parts of the palace; but George III disliked Hampton Court, and from that time onward the palace became a royal museum.

WINDSOR CASTLE

William the Conqueror built a castle here, a thousand years ago; and Henry I converted it into a palace. But nothing remains of their work. The present castle is a mixture of mediaeval and Georgian styles. Between 1356 and 1361 William of Wykeham was Clerk of the Works. Henry III added three towers; Edward III demolished much of the early building, and raised the Round Tower. Three Kings built St George's Chapel—Edward VI, Henry VII, Henry VIII. Queen Elizabeth added the north terrace; Charles II renovated the State Apartments; George IV employed Jeffrey Wyatt to make extensive changes and additions (1824-40).

Windsor Castle is the oldest of all the royal homes. It serves admirably as a country seat within easy reach of the capital. Across the river stands Eton College, another royal foundation, created by Henry VI.

REIGATE MILL

In 1069 there were thousands of windmills at work in England; in 1969 there were less than thirty. Not every windmill was used to grin corn; some adapted themselves to paper, gunpower, metal. The phrase 'thumb of gold' recalls the miller's custom of taking one-tenth of the flour as his payment. Chaucer's Reeve had nothing good to say of such a fellow:

> *He felt it with his thumb, and thus he knew*
> *Its quality, and took three times his due.*

Hilaire Belloc lamented the decay of his favourite Ha'nacker Mill:

> *Ha'nacker's down and England's done.*

Reigate Mill is more fortunate, for it belongs to the National Trust, which owns several other properties here—Reigate Old Town Hall, Reigate Heath, the Priory, St Mary's Church. It is good to find a country scene, only twenty-two miles from London.

THE SEVEN SISTERS

These famous chalk cliffs are best seen from Seaford Head. Sussex folk call them Haven Brow, Short Brow, Rough Brow, Bran Point, Flagstaff Point, Baily's Point, West Brow Hill. Much of the coastline belongs to the National Trust.

If stone could speak, the Seven Sisters would tell of Roman legions, of Saxon pirates, Norman knights, Spanish galleons, French privateers, skies loud with German bombers and English Spitfires, and the Royal Navy on watch against the enemy's unlawful occasions. And the Sisters might have a word also about smugglers, bringing 'baccy for the parson, brandy for the squire, and a packet of tea for the farmer's wife. In summertime the roads inland are crammed with cars, but in spring and winter you may walk the cliffs all day alone, hearing only the gulls and the wind and the waves.

ALFRISTON, SUSSEX

The fourteenth-century church of St Andrew is known locally as the Cathedral of the Downs. Certainly it is high, airy, spacious. Nearby stands the former clergy-house (*c.*1350), a tiny wattle-and-daub hall, beside a green mound or Tye (Old English *teag* or enclosure). This clergy-house was the first English property to be acquired by the National Trust.

The centre of Alfriston is a market place with some remains of a mediaeval Cross. The narrow High Street is flanked by many venerable houses and shops; the Star Inn, for example, was built five centuries ago. A miniature museum contains some endearing relics of the not-so-distant past, including a gramophone and a radio set of the 1920s. The Congregational Church was founded four years before the Battle of Trafalgar. Above and about, the Downs stand guard; and a footbridge spans the River Cuckmere.

POYNINGS, SUSSEX

Sussex people call this village 'Punnings'. In the year 1381 Michael Poynings, lord of the manor, was responsible for the defence of the Sussex shore. Sir Edward Poynings achieved fame as Henry VII's deputy in Ireland. His so-called 'Poynings' Law' defined constitutional procedure among the Irish. The family mansion was destroyed by fire in 1727.

Founded by Michael Poynings in 1369 to replace a Norman church, the church of the Holy Trinity is built chiefly of chalk and dressed flints. Several members of the Poynings family are buried in the church. Despite its nearness to Brighton, the village remains relatively unspoiled, as though the Downs had shielded it against Mammon. Andrew Young knew this high land, and found

Primroses thick on its steep floor.

PETWORTH HOUSE, SUSSEX

The first mansion belonged to the mediaeval Percys, from whom it passed by marriage to a seventeenth-century Duke of Somerset who demolished much of the old house, and created the present magnificence (the name of the architect is unknown).

Petworth House is a monument to English artistry and craftsmanship before mass-production. Grinling Gibbons, for example, carved one of the rooms with birds, fruit, animals, flowers. There is a Van Dyck Room, a Beauty Room, a Marble Hall (whose carpet was made at Exeter in 1758). Many of the pictures were acquired by a northern nobleman, the third Earl of Egremont; they include works by Turner, Romney, Lely, Gainsborough, Reynolds, Hals, Holbein, Rembrandt, Lorraine, Van Dyck. Petworth House today is the seat of another northern peer, Lord Leconfield. Its park—ten miles around—is open to the public on certain days.

BODIAM CASTLE, SUSSEX

Bodiam is a castle without a history, for it arose at the end of the Middle Ages, when the fortified manor was supplanting the military castle. Its first owner was Sir Edward Dalyngruge—Custodian of the Tower, and Governor of the City of London—who built the castle in order to protect the upper reaches of the River Rother.

Bodiam is about 180 feet square, with walls six feet thick, within which the apartments were set around a courtyard. The turrets on the twin-towered gatehouse were stepped-out so that molten lead could be poured upon any attackers. Two centuries ago Grose described the castle as a romantic ruin: 'This venerable structure, whose mouldering towers and rugged walls . . . afford at once a most picturesque subject for the pencil . . .'. The castle has been renovated by the National Trust, to which it was given by Lord Curzon.

CANTERBURY CATHEDRAL

Built in the shape of a double cross, Canterbury Cathedral is 522 feet long. Its amalgam of styles, from Norman to Perpendicular, recalls the earlier churches here, destroyed by fire. During the twelfth century the chief architect was a Frenchman, William of Sens, who was succeeded by William the Englishman, designer of the east crypt and Trinity chapel. Between 1376 and 1410 the nave of an earlier church was replaced. Cardinal Morton's central tower arose during the fifteenth century.

The cathedral was damaged by the rebels during the Civil War, by fire in 1872, and by bombs during the last war. A fourteenth-century compromise kept the peace between north and south by styling the Archbishop of York as the Primate of England, and the Archbishop of Canterbury as the Primate of All England.

CANTERBURY CATHEDRAL, INTERIOR

Canterbury is the *burg* or town of the *Cantware* or men of Kent. During the later Middle Ages it was England's foremost shrine, attracting pilgrims throughout Christendom, both pedestrians and horsemen (whence the word 'canter'). Chaucer wrote:

> *. . . from every shires ende*
> *Of Englelonde to Caunterbury they wende.*

These pilgrims came to revere the memory of Thomas A' Becket, Henry II's turbulent friend, who was consecrated Archbishop only twenty-four hours after he had been ordained priest. Having challenged the secular power, he was murdered in the cathedral by four knights. His shrine was dismantled when Henry VIII issued a writ, accusing him of treason and contumacy. Having been dead for nearly four centuries, the prisoner was unable to appear. Celia Fiennes admired the mediaeval glass: 'An art', she sighed, 'which now is lost among us.'

PENSHURST, KENT

Penshurst means the hurst or wood belonging to Pefen. It used to be called Spenshurst. When Celia Fiennes came here she wrote: '. . . there is a good seat of Lord Lesters, Spenshurst, which stands in a very good parke . . . with a good hall and gallery full of good old pictures.'

This was the birthplace (1544) of Sir Philip Sidney, soldier, diplomat, courtier, poet, who was mortally wounded at the siege of Zutphen ('Thy need is greater than mine'). In his day the house was a centre of learning. Ben Jonson stayed here, and wrote a poem praising the host who honoured artists:

> *The same beer, and bread, and self-same wine,*
> *That is his lordship's, shall be mine.*

Penshurst has belonged to the Sidney family since 1522; the present owner, Viscount De L'isle and Dudley, is a collateral descendant of Sir Philip Sidney.

CHICHESTER CATHEDRAL

To the Romans the city of Chichester was *Noviomagus*; to the Saxons it became the camp of Cissa. Bishop Ralph de Luffa founded the cathedral during the twelfth century. In 1186 it was damaged by fire; in 1199 the rebuilding was consecrated by Bishop Seffrid. The east end was enlarged during the thirteenth century; the Chapter House and the great window in the south transept were added by Bishop Langton during the fourteenth century.

In 1861 the spire on the central tower collapsed and was restored by Sir Gilbert Scott, to a height of 277 feet. Chichester is the only English cathedral with a detached bell tower (two of its eight bells were cast by John Wallis at Salisbury in 1583 and 1587). The north transept contains memorials to two composers, Thomas Weelkes (1625) and Gustav Holst (1924). Defoe thought that the approach to Chichester Cathedral was '. . . the most pleasant beautiful country in England'.

CHILBOLTON, HAMPSHIRE

A thousand years ago this place was called Ceoldboldingtun or the home of Ceolbeald's people. Who Ceobeald was we do not know and probably never shall. Certainly his old home has never hit the headlines of history. But how gentle and fertile was his land, and how much more so it has become after a thousand years of cultivation.

When Ceobeald arrived, the district was densely wooded, haunted by deer and wild boars. Now it is rich farmland, watered by many chalk streams, made companionable by half-timbered houses. Notice, too, the perennial harvest of daffodils, first sown by a lover of the land. To a botanist the flower is *Narcissus pseudonarcissus L,* but our fathers coined a lovelier name, Daffy-Down-Dilly.

SALISBURY CATHEDRAL

In 1220 the Bishop of Salisbury laid one foundation stone for the Pope, one for Stephen Langton, and a third for himself. Within thirty-eight years the cathedral was complete, except for the spire. Now it covers an area of 55,000 square feet, and the spire reaches 404 feet above the lawns.

In 1668 an architect discovered that the spire was leaning. His report —in faded ink—may be seen in the cathedral library, with a note by one of the clergy: 'The Estate of the Cathedral Church of St Mary, Sarum, represented and the Defects enumerated by the most ingenious and worthy Dr Christopher Wren, August 31st, 1668.' Two centuries later Sir George Gilbert Scott reported: 'Though the spire has stood so long, there is nothing to ensure against failure at any moment . . .'. But Salisbury spire prevails, under expert surveillance.

STONEHENGE

Stonehenge is Europe's greatest monument to pre-history. We know approximately when it was built—between 1900 and 1500 BC—but precisely how, and exactly why, we do not know, and probably never shall. Geologists have proved that some of the stones came from the Prescelly Hills in Pembrokeshire. But how did they arrive? Were they hauled all the way by an army of men and beasts? Or were they ferried across the Severn Sea, or over its upper estuary? Two facts are beyond dispute; those semi-savages built Stonehenge to be some kind of religious centre, and their alignment of its stones reveals an astute knowledge of astronomy.

In 1915 Stonehenge was sold for £6,600 to Sir Cecil Chubb, who in 1918 gave it to the nation. Here, like Siegfried Sassoon, you feel the touch of

> *Time, that anticipates eternities,*
> *And has an art to resurrect the rose.*

WELLS CATHEDRAL

Many good judges rate the west front of Wells Cathedral as the loveliest spiritual architecture in Britain. There has been a church here ever since King Ina founded a shrine for his Saxon subjects. The present cathedral arose between the twelfth and the thirteenth centuries. Around its greensward are set the Vicar's Close, the Bishop's Barn, the Deanery, the Penniless Porch, the Cloisters. The Bishop's Palace was begun by Jocelin seven centuries ago; set in a quadrangle, and surrounded by a huge wall, it is the most impressive of all our priestly palaces.

The interior of the cathedral contains many statues and tombs of famous men; yet it was, and is still, a place of worship for the unknown men whom Edmund Blunden remembered:

> *From this church they led their brides,*
> *From this church themselves were led*
> *Shoulder-high; on these waysides*
> *Sat to take their beer and bread.*

CHAGFORD, DEVON

Chagford is the ford of gorse (Old English *ceacge*) by the River Teign. This little town became a Stannary centre in 1328. The Three Crowns Inn was a mediaeval monastery. The church—dedicated to St Catherine, patroness of miners—has a processional Cross made from the metal of a Zeppelin that was shot down in 1916.

All around, the hills of Devonshire rise up like unwearied eagles. Some of the land is moor, some pasture, some arable. Everywhere the hedges and trees civilize this outpost of Dartmoor; and at ploughing time the red earth creates a regional rubric. Celia Fiennes set the scene: '. . . on these hills as I said one can discern little besides inclosures hedges and trees, rarely can see houses unless you are just descending to them, they always are placed in holes as it were . . .'

BLACKPOOL SANDS, DEVON

Most unlike Lancashire's Blackpool: inland a little, the narrow streets of Stoke Fleming climb steeply above Start Bay. For centuries the church tower was a seaman's pilot to the fairway through Dartmouth harbour.

A lane winds downhill, past a thatched barn, to Blackpool Sands, an idyll of pastures sloping to a horse-shoe beach. Unlike the more majestic north coast of Devon, this Channel shore is gentle. Its cliffs slither leisurely, and are fringed with hedges and trees and flowers. The Sands are untainted by lollipops, car parks, tea shacks. Even in December you may sometimes lie here in the sun, listening to the lark; and when March arrives, you will find the primroses daubing the lanes with drops of sunshine. R. D. Blackmore spoke the truth when he said that Devon was '. . . the fairest county in England'.

BICKLEIGH, DEVON

Bickleigh lies on the River Exe near Tiverton. Its five-arched bridge gazes admiringly at a cluster of white houses and amber thatch, crowned with innumerable flowers. Every cottage is a nest of birds, the same that John Clare saw in his native Shires:

> *The sparrow, too, their daily guest,*
> *Is in the cottage eaves at rest . . .*

Bickleigh Court, hidden among trees, has for centuries been the seat of the Carews, one of whom fought at Flodden Field. Several members of the family were 'squarsons', and one served as priest for half a century. Bickleigh would have pleased Robert Herrick, who prized the seclusion of his own Devon parsonage:

> *We blesse our Fortunes, when we see*
> *Our own beloved privacie . . .*

BRIXHAM HARBOUR, DEVON

Brixham has known many glorious hours. Here berthed Sir Francis Drake, bearing with him a galleon which he had captured from the Spanish Armada. Here, a century later, landed William of Orange, pretender to the Stuart throne. Here, on 7th August, 1815—within sight of the Quay—ex-Emperor Napoleon Bonaparte embarked in *HMS Northumberland,* outward bound for exile and death on St Helena. Here the vicar of All Saints', Henry Francis Lyte, wrote *Abide with Me* (and when Nurse Edith Cavell faced the German firing squad, she recited the last stanza of that hymn).

Between 1890 and 1914 the famous Brixham trawlers enjoyed their heydays; gaff-rigged, with a main boom nearly sixty feet long. Nowadays a dwindling fishing fleet is outnumbered by the colourful occasions of holiday boatfolk.

TRELISSICK, CORNWALL

This is the Roseland Riviera—Cornish *ros*, meaning a heath or wild place—long since tamed by tillage and the craftsmanship that built Trelissick, a neo-Greek mansion, designed *c.*1825 by P. F. Robinson. Its grounds delve greenly to the blue and blended water of the Fal and Truro rivers.

Here a salt-water compass is boxed by saintly villages: St Just, St Michael, St Clement, St Day, and—loveliest of them all—St Anthony-in-Roseland. This was the country of Sir Arthur Quiller-Couch, sometime Mayor of Fowey and Professor of English Literature, who praised his Duchy in prose and verse, and the flowers that he had planted there:

> *Bless them, the violets,*
> *Bless me, the gardener,*
> *Bless thee, the giver.*

BODMIN MOOR, CORNWALL

Overlooked by Brown Willy, Cornwall's highest hill, the Moor pursues its own ways, ignoring a loud main road. Northward lie Camelford and the Atlantic; southward, the Luxulyan valley, lush as its Cornish name (*Lan Solian* or Sulian's monastery). Camelford claims to be the scene of a battle in which King Arthur met Medrawd:

> *Striking the last stroke with Excalibur,*
> *Slew him, and, all but slain himself, he fell.*

At Dozemary Pool, they say, in the heart of the Moor, Sir Bedivere reluctantly obeyed the King's command to hurl Excalibur into the water. But all that was long ago and faraway. Bodmin Moor today is a rain-rinsed, mist-marooned island of fey and farms, known only to those who follow its lanes and zany tracks.

HELFORD RIVER, CORNWALL

The Romans built small camps on Helford River, and very likely used the place as a harbour for exporting Cornish tin. When Defoe arrived in 1726 he found '. . . a small, but good harbour . . . where many times the TINN ships go to load for London: also here are a good number of fishing vessels for the pilchard trade . . .' There is no fishing fleet now; neither ships nor harbour; only an arm of the sea, running the gauntlet of green woods that sweep the surface gently. Sometimes a house peeps out from among the trees; and a waterside inn offers a good tie-up for yachtsmen.

Happy indeed the man who plies his craft around the Cornish coast. But there is a mighty rock hereabouts, waiting to devour the starboard quarter of any vessel bearing too close as she enters the River from St Mawes.

LAND'S END, CORNWALL

When Daniel Defoe saw the waves beating against the rocks at Land's End he was moved to write: 'Nature has thus fortify'd this part of the island of Britain in a strange manner . . . as if she knew the force and violence of the mighty ocean.' This is the most dreaded sector of the English coast. Even a modern steamer gives it a wide berth, warned by the Longships Lighthouse. Swinburne remembered the schooners that listened anxiously

> *To the loud rocks and surging reaches home*
> *That take the wild wrath of the Cornish foam.*

Twilight and dawn are the visiting hours, for then fact breeds with fey to beget poetry. Westward, they say, lies Lyonesse, that legendary land, sunken in sand. North-east, King Arthur's Tintagel clings to its cliff. Here, centuries later, eyes scanned the skyline for a Great Armada and for that greater Armada which swept-in from the clouds.

MERTON COLLEGE, OXFORD

Founded by Walter de Merton, Bishop of Rochester, in 1264, this is the third oldest college in Oxford, and the first to become residential. Among its sons were Sir Thomas Bodley (donor of the great library), Mr Speaker Lenthall, Sir William Harvey (he discovered the circulation of the blood), Richard Steele, Lord Randolph Churchill, Andrew Lang, Edmund Blunden.

Merton gatehouse was built in 1418; much of the rest was rebuilt by Sir Henry Saville a hundred years later. The college chapel contains glass from the thirteenth century. Merton Street is a cobbled backwater of gracious houses, sheltered from the commercial clangour of the High. Alongside are Merton gardens, bounded by remains of the mediaeval city wall; and beyond them the meadows.

CHRIST CHURCH, OXFORD

Oxford men call this The House because it was known as *Aedes Christi* or Christ's House—though its founder, Cardinal Wolsey, was an ungodly fellow whose pride fell before he could complete his project. Even the briefest litany of Christ Church men reads like a history of England, for it enrolls a Prince of Wales (Edward VII) and eleven premiers (including Gladstone, Canning, and Sir Robert Peel).

Peckwater Quadrangle was designed by Dean Aldrich; Canterbury Quadrangle by James Wyatt; Tom Tower by Sir Christopher Wren (it houses the Great Bell from Osney Abbey). But the chief glory is the Hall that Matthew Arnold's Scholar Gipsy saw when he

> *Turn'd once to watch, while thick the snowflakes fall,*
> *The line of festal lights in Christ Church Hall . . .*

BLENHEIM PALACE, OXFORDSHIRE

On 13th August, 1704, the Duke of Marlborough defeated the French at the battle of Blenheim. Next day—on the back of an officer's wine bill—he pencilled a note to his wife: 'I have not time to say more but beg you will give my duty to the Queen and let her know her army has had a glorious victory.' The nation showed its gratitude by building Blenheim Palace for him and his heirs for ever. When the Duke died, only the east wing was complete; that the rest ever did get built was due to the indomitable Sarah, Dowager Duchess of Marlborough.

Sir Christopher Wren submitted a design, but was displaced by Sir John Vanburgh. The Palace itself covers three acres. The park of 2,500 acres was laid out by Capability Brown. Nearby, at Bladon, another grateful generation buried another great Churchill.

LOWER SLAUGHTER, GLOUCESTERSHIRE

There is nothing macabre in this bloody-sounding hamlet; but in winter its Cotswold stream may overflow, whence the name (Old English *sloughtre* or slough). Nothing has ever happened here, except the only important happenings . . . birth and burial, love and hatred, sorrow and joy, failure and success. Lower Slaughter is among those hamlets which Thomas Hardy described as a '. . . one-eyed, blinking sort of place'.

Every house is a gem; that is, of precious stone, made-to-measure by men who assumed that necessity needs not to be a synonym for ugliness. These houses will abide when the Building Societies have had to rebuild themselves. John Drinkwater set the scene to music:

> *I see the barns and comely manors planned*
> *By men who somehow moved in comely thought,*
> *Who, with a simple shippon on their hands,*
> *As men upon some godlike business wrought . . .*

THE COTSWOLDS

The Cotswolds are commonly taken to be a hilly region of Oxfordshire and Gloucestershire, but the phrase would be more properly used to define parts of Warwickshire, Oxfordshire, Gloucestershire, Worcestershire, Wiltshire, in which a type of stone is found. This stone is called Oolite (two Greek words, meaning 'egg' and 'stone') because the egg-shaped lumps of calcium carbonate do resemble a fish's roe. There are two kinds of Oolite—Great and Inferior—the latter being sometimes as bright as an orange. No other region of England contains so many and such consistently handsome houses, churches, barns.

This vista shows the border between Gloucestershire and Worcestershire, with Dumbleton Hill in the middle distance. From the hills beyond, the Malverns and the Welsh mountains are visible.

CHIPPING CAMPDEN, GLOUCESTERSHIRE

Chipping Campden—the *chipping* or market at the *campadenu* or fortified valley—is the queen of the Cotswolds, a benediction of beautiful buildings. Celia Fiennes was entranced: '. . . its built all of Stone as is its Church which is pretty, for such a little town its large . . .'. In that church lies Baptist Hicks, first Viscount Campden. The present viscounty is a courtesy title borne by the re-created earldom of Gainsborough (1841). In 1929 the Campden Trust was formed to defend the town against Mammon and his fellow-traveller, Progress.

The Wonder of Chipping Campden was William Harrison, who disappeared in 1660, but returned two years later, when his three 'murderers' had been hanged. In 1906 John Masefield wrote a play about this, *The Campden Wonder*.

NORTH COTSWOLDS

Here you are on Fish Hill, at the edge of the western ridge above Broadway and the Vale of Evesham in Worcestershire. Said Jane Austen, 'Many counties, I believe, are called the Garden of England.' This county deserves that name. Are not Evesham and Pershore famed for their orchards? And is not Worcestershire a centre for hop-growing?

Grapes, too, grew hereabouts; notably at Hailes Abbey, founded by Richard, Earl of Cornwall—brother to Henry III—in thanksgiving for his escape from shipwreck. It may seem strange that grapes should have flourished on these hills, but a vine will withstand several degrees of frost. These northern Cotswolds are a vantage-point for all who would

> *. . . see the coloured counties,*
> *And hear the larks so high*
> *About us in the sky.*

DUNTISBOURNE ROUS, GLOUCESTERSHIRE

There are three Duntisbournes, each within a few miles of the others: Duntisbourne Leer, Duntisbourne Abbots (it belonged to Gloucester Abbey), and Duntisbourne Rous (in 1285 the manor was held by a red-haired Norman, Roger le Rus, from the French *roux* or red). Watered by a stream, this hamlet contains a few farms and one miniature church whose Norman walls show traces of Saxon herringbone work. It has, too, a crypt—a rarity in so small a place—and a saddleback tower.

Some villages grew large with the centuries; others dwindled; a few disappeared. Duntisbourne Rous was born small, and has stayed that way. Happy the man who came here in Ralph Hodgson's springtime

> *When every sky was blue, and rain*
> *And sudden rainbows in between,*
> *And every bough in leaf again,*
> *And all the world was gold and green.*

BURFORD, OXFORDSHIRE

Burford, or the ford by a hill, the queen of the Oxfordshire Cotswolds: a steep High Street is flanked by houses from the Middle Ages to the last century. The ancient Tolsey or Customs House perches on pillars. This picture shows Sheep Street and its two sixteenth-century hotels (the manorial offices of *The Countryman* are nearby). Here, too, Garne's ancient brewery is still powered by the steam-engine that was built by a Burford millwright in 1870. Burford Priory used to be the home of a Tudor Chief Baron of the Exchequer, Sir Lawrence Tanfield.

At the foot of High Street, on the banks of the Windrush, Burford church is as large as a small cathedral. Andrew Lang was right when he called this

> *A land of waters green and clear,*
> *Of willows and of poplars tall . . .*

GLOUCESTER CATHEDRAL

In 1089 the men of Gloucester laid the foundations of an abbey, in which King Henry III was crowned. Successive abbots rebuilt and enlarged the church, adding the south transept in 1335, and the central tower in 1450. At the Reformation the Benedictine monks were ejected, and their abbey became a cathedral. The east window—seventy-two feet high—is said to have been given c.1350 by Lord Bradeston, in memory of Sir Maurice Berkeley, a Gloucestershire man, who fell at the siege of Calais.

The cathedral has monuments to another Gloucestershire worthy, Dr Edward Jenner (the pioneer of vaccination) and to a composer, Sir Hubert Parry. Two poets were educated at the Crypt Grammar School; one was John Taylor; the other—and better—was W. E. Henley, who believed that

Life is good, and joy runs high
Between English earth and sky.

NEAR SHEPSCOMBE, GLOUCESTERSHIRE

Shep, of course, means sheep; and sheep mean rich meadows and rich merchants. This snowscape, worthy of Breughel himself, shows a typical Cotswold combe, with food and fodder for the stock. Defoe noted the fertility of these parts: 'Gloucestershire', he wrote, 'must not be pass'd over, without some account of a most pleasant and fruitful vale which crosses part of the country . . .'.

The Cotswold breed of sheep can be traced back to the fourteenth century, when the English wool trade was laying the foundations of national wealth. (The Lord Chancellor sits on a Woolsack, to symbolise the economic importance of fleece.) During the nineteenth century the Cotswold breed was crossed with Leicesters, but in 1818 a survey for the Board of Agriculture reported that some of the original stock still flourished: '. . . the opinion is in favour of a cross with the new Leicester, though pure Cotswold sheep are still to be found on several farms.'

FOTHERINGHAY, NORTHAMPTONSHIRE

The lane from Oundle crosses the River Nene within sight of a surging church and the green mound where a castle stood. Now only its site remains. In that castle Richard III was born, and Mary Queen of Scots was beheaded. An eye-witness said that the Queen met her death '... apparalled in a kinde of joye'. There was a great college at Fotheringhay, founded by Edmund de Langley, son of Edward III, but a fire destroyed it (and parts of the church also) during Edward VI's reign.

The village itself is remote, restful, unmarred by modernity. Some of the houses incorporate part of the inns which received mediaeval visitors to the castle and college. In this county of spires and squires, the wooded pastures contemplate the eternal verities, and you may wander among them for hours without disturbing their meditations.

A HUNTING SCENE

Hunting is part of an English countryman's life. He hunts hares, pheasants, rabbits, fish, deer, otters, partridges, pigeons. But his chief quarry is the fox; so, 'hunting' has come to mean fox-hunting. In 1969 there were more than two hundred packs of fox-hounds in Britain—an increase of twenty per cent on the number during the late nineteenth century.

Here the Quorn Pack meets at Luvesby Park in Leicestershire; the covert on the horizon is called Diamond Spinney. The word Quorn (Old English *cweorn* or millstone) means 'a hill where millstones are found'. The epic of fox-hunting is John Masefield's *Reynard the Fox*. Do you remember the lullaby of Robin the Huntsman?

> *The horses in stable loved their straw.*
> *"Good-night, my beauties", said Robin Dawe.*

WORCESTER CATHEDRAL

Worcester used to be a quiet country town. Now it has become a loud industrial city, top-heavy with factory chimneys and skyscraping offices. Amidst all this scurry, the cathedral invites the visitor to follow Stephen Spender's advice:

> *Never to allow the traffic to smother*
> *With noise and fog the flowering of the spirit.*

Worcester first became a city in 880, but was razed by the Danes and then rebuilt when King Alfred held a Witan here. In 983 Bishop Oswald founded a new cathedral, which the Danes again destroyed. The present building was dedicated by Bishop Sylvester in the presence of Henry III. Here King John was buried. The Deanery used to be the Bishop's Palace. Henry VIII endowed a Cathedral School (Samuel Butler was among its pupils). Celia Fiennes found the cathedral '. . . a lofty magnificent building . . .'.

SHAKESPEARE'S BIRTHPLACE

How little we know of the world's supreme poet. His father was the town ale-taster; his wife was Anne Hathaway, by whom he had a daughter, Judith. At school he smattered 'small Latin and less Greek'. Then he migrated to London, became an actor, wrote some plays, returned to Stratford, bought himself a gentleman's residence (which he rebuilt and named New Place), acquired a grant of arms (with the motto *non sanz droict*), and then died. We have no certain portrait of him, no letter, no priceless poem in his own hand. Others abide our questions, but he, the greatest, is too distant even to be approached.

Nevertheless, this unknown man is famous throughout the world; and the world comes to visit his homeland, which he was proud to call

This precious stone, set in the silver sea,
This blessed plot, this earth, this realm, this England.

CHADDESLEY CORBETT, WORCESTERSHIRE

Here is a twice-blessed village, for it lies off the main road, and is restful in its own right; set in a countryside whose best parts still tally with Celia Fiennes' description: '. . . a Country of Gardens and Orchards, the whole Country being very full of fruite trees. . . .' Two centuries later, as we have seen, the same countryside was sung by A. E. Housman:

Here of a Sunday morning
My love and I would lie,
And see the coloured counties,
And hear the larks so high . . .

The story of Chaddesley is partly told by its second name, for the Corbet family held the manor from the twelfth century until 1359, when it passed to several other families—Beauchamps, Lisles, Dudleys —and in 1529 was bought by the Pakingtons of Hampton Lovett.

GREAT COMBERTON, WORCESTERSHIRE

Comberton, or the village in a combe, is Great only in comparison with villages that are even smaller. Whether Shakespeare himself ever came here we do not know: *n'importe,* for this secluded place is in many ways a replica of the other Warwickshire villages which Shakespeare did know. His plays abound in praise of the English countryside.

Weary of their 'hollow crown', his Kings dream that they are shepherds; and the King's subjects walk always with a hand upon their hilt, swift to draw in defence of

This royal throne of kings, this scepter'd isle . . .

Possibly at Great Comberton, certainly at some similar village, Shakespeare wandered in lilac-time, and said to himself:

Merrily, merrily shall I live now
Under the blossom that hangs on the bough.

FINCHINGFIELD, ESSEX

This Essex village never was a field of finches; its name means 'the open country belonging to Finc or his people'. Even fifty years ago it was a deep country; now it is a semi-suburb of London, though happily unspoiled by 'development'.

Finchingfield parish was so extensive that several great families held parts of it—Clare, Vere, Marshal—and its importance was emphasised by a famous manor Spain's Hall, a moated Tudor mansion. As this picture reveals, the Norman tower of the church of St John the Baptist is crowned by an eighteenth-century cupola. The water in the foreground looks like a pond, but is part of a stream flowing through the village. This is the corner of England which Edmund Blunden loved:

> *From all these happy folk I find*
> *Life's radiance kindle in my mind . . .*

HATFIELD HOUSE, HERTFORDSHIRE

Toward the end of the Middle Ages a family of Welsh gentlemen anglicised their name from Sitsyllt to Cecil. Under the Welsh Tudor dynasty the Cecils advanced. They became Roman Catholics in order to please Queen Mary, and Protestants in order not to displease Queen Elizabeth. William Cecil—by this time Lord Burghley—served Queen Elizabeth for forty years.

Hatfield House was built by William's son, Robert Cecil, first Earl of Exeter, who died before it had been finished. Shaped like the letter E, as a compliment to the Queen, the House is among the most palatial in the kingdom. Its Long Gallery is 150 yards from end to end; the Park, watered by the River Lea, covers 1,300 acres, and is seven miles around. Among the family treasures are the death warrant of Mary Queen of Scots and a diary in which Lord Burghley recorded the defeat of the Spanish Armada.

WIVENHOE, ESSEX

When Celia Fiennes explored the eastern parts of England she approved the '. . . sight of so many neate villages with rows of trees about them and very neate built Churches sometimes 5 or 6 of these are in view together in 3 or four mile of each other . . . .' Wivenhoe certainly is neat; and so is its church.

Hoe is a common name hereabouts, meaning a spur or spit of land. This is a region of rivers and salt water estuaries; a land of amphibious men who can take a fish with as much ease as they snare a rabbit or wing a partridge. Their commercial traffic dwindled when steam appeared, and died when petrol was born. But the sea is in our veins, and the Essex inshoremen ply a brisk trade among holiday yachtsmen.

KERSEY, SUFFOLK

Daniel Defoe was impressed by Suffolk's scientific farming: 'This part of England', he declared, 'is also remarkable for being the first where the feeding and fattening of cattle, (both sheep as well as black cattle) with turnips was first practis'd in England . . . .' But Suffolk had waxed rich on wool long before turnips became a staple diet. Kersey is a notable example of that prosperity. The streets slope down both sides of a valley; red-brick or half-timbered, the houses paint times past. One of them, Sampson's Hall, recalls the name of the man who owned it in 1381.

On a knoll overlooking the village, the church makes a spectacular claim upon attention. Priory Farm contains parts of a twelfth-century Austin Priory. All around, the pastures are grazed by prime cattle and plump sheep.

CAMBRIDGE, THE BACKS

Despite some factories, Cambridge retains its identity as a University and a country town. The first residential college, Peterhouse, was opened in 1284, but formal recognition did not arrive until 1318, when King Edward II asked Pope John XXII to issue a Bull whereby the colleges became each a *studium generale* with the privileges of a *Universitas*. Thereafter the University ceased to lie within the jurisdiction of the Bishop, and a Cambridge doctor could lecture anywhere in Christendom.

One of the loveliest jewels in the Light Blue crown is its river, the Cam, which flows beside several college gardens, so creating a waterscape known as 'the Backs'. Come here at daffodil time, when bare and budding branches offer venerable vistas: and come, if you can, at sunrise, for then, like Wordsworth, you will stand

Alone, beneath this fairy work of earth.

CAMBRIDGE, THE BACKS

Trinity's eighteenth-century bridge, and St John's nineteenth-century New Court: in summer the River Cam is punt-plied by youth that has lately shed the penultimate skin of adolescence, and now proposes to perfect the world sometime next month.

Cam is a Celtic river-name, related to the Welsh *cam* or 'crooked'. The Cam rises at Ashwell in Hertfordshire, and then flows forty miles northward to join the Ouse near Ely. At Grantchester the River Granta chimes in, flowing up from Essex. In 1912, shortly before he became a Fellow of King's, Rupert Brooke—on holiday in Berlin—was seized with a sudden longing for home:

> *. . . would I were*
> *In Grantchester, in Grantchester!*

ALDEBURGH, SUFFOLK

The name Aldeburgh, or *alde burh,* means 'old fort'. In theory the place is a hotch-potch, chiefly Victorian and Edwardian; in practice it is an endearing coastal village with a lifeboat, a fifteenth-century Moot Hall (restored 1855), and a sun dial (1650) whose Latin motto invites our own hours to become serene.

Three famous people lived at Aldeburgh: Benjamin Britten, the composer, who sponsored an annual music festival here; Elizabeth Garrett Anderson, one of the earliest English women doctors (her husband founded Aldeburgh golf club in 1907); and the Rev. George Crabbe, a native of the place, who made it the hero (and sometimes the villain) of his poetry:

> *Dabbling on shore half-naked sea-boys crowd,*
> *Swim round the ship, or swing upon a shroud . . .*

IPSWICH, SUFFOLK

Ipswich was anciently *Gipeswic,* the *wic* or settlement at the *gip* or mouth of the River Orwell. Ipswich, in short, is a harbour. When Defoe arrived he found four hundred ships lying here '. . . as safe as in a wet dock'. The mediaeval harbour thrived by importing French wine and by exporting English cloth; thereafter it specialised in exporting corn and coal. Much of the old town—or such of it as survives—lies by the water.

William Smart endowed the Town Library in 1599; the Presbyterian chapel (afterwards Unitarian) was built a century later. Only a redbrick gateway recalls the College which Cardinal Wolsey founded in 1528, shortly before his downfall (tradition says that Wolsey himself was the son of an Ipswich butcher). Now the town is an industrial area with a population of 100,000, overspilling into adjacent villages.

PETERBOROUGH, NORTHAMPTONSHIRE

Peterborough was long ago marred by pylons, factories, and commercial travellers. In that prosperous desert the cathedral abides like an oasis of sanity. King Edgar built an abbey here, which was burned down in 1166, and replaced by the present church (it became a cathedral after the Reformation).

Visitors should obtain permission to climb the tower, which offers a memorable view of the triforium. The timbered Norman roof must be unique in Britain; an Early English west front was added c.1210. Queen Katherine of Aragon was buried here; so also was Mary Queen of Scots (to be re-interred at Westminster Abbey by command of her son, James First and Sixth). Those two royal ladies were buried by Old Scarlett, a sexton, whose memorial adorns the west wall.

THE NORFOLK BROADS

The Norfolk Broads offer halcyon days to inland mariners. Centuries ago these lakes formed a vast estuary. Now they are a brackish blend of freshwater and brine, haunted by heron, water-hen, kingfisher, bittern, snipe. In all, they cover some five thousand acres, seldom more than nine feet deep, linked by several rivers, including the Yare, the Waveney, and the Bure.

The largest of the Broads is Breydon Water (1,200 acres). Especially popular among yachtsmen and cabin-cruisers are Wroxham Broad (100 acres) near Norwich, Ranworth Broad (120 acres) and the Great and Little Broads of Hoveton (200 acres together). Barton Broad (270 acres) is fed by the River Ant, which Nelson knew because it rises near his old school, Paston Grammar School, at North Walsham. Charles Kingsley loved these East Anglian skyscrapes. Here, he said, '. . . the arch of heaven spreads more ample than elsewhere . . .'.

OXBURGH HALL, NORFOLK

King Henry VII slept here, in a room whose linenfold panelling has mellowed with the years. Sir Edmund Bedingfield built the Hall, soon after the Wars of the Roses; and Bedingfields have occupied it ever since, except during Cromwell's dictatorship, when the rebels stole the Hall and sold it to the highest bidder. In 1513 Margaret Bedingfield built a chapel in the parish church nearby. The family is one of the oldest in East Anglia; from c.1309 a branch resided at Fleming's Hall in Suffolk.

Oxburgh Hall stands in a park, through which the River Wissey flows. A moat reflects the embattled walls, carved chimneys, stepped gables. The gatehouse is topped by two towers, seven storeys high; and the Hall itself overlooks a great courtyard.

NORWICH CATHEDRAL

Celia Fiennes, that ubiquitously observant traveller, found this '. . . a fine large Cathedral and very lofty . . .'. A century later, James Woodforde, himself a parson, praised the sermons as '. . . very sensible and sound . . .'.

Norwich has been styled the City of Churches; once it possessed fifty; even now it retains more than thirty. The cathedral itself was founded in 1096 by Bishop Herbert de Losingas. Its tower, three hundred and fifteen feet high, is second only to Salisbury's. The library contains the famous Berners book, printed by Wynkyn de Worde, Caxton's foreman. Nurse Edith Cavell, daughter of a Norfolk parson, is buried in Life's Green near the east end. Robert Louis Stevenson was justified when he said: 'Men are never so happy as when they build a cathedral.'

FARNDALE, YORKSHIRE

Farndale, or the dale of ferns, is best viewed from the hill beside Gila-moor Church, on whose wall you will find an inscribed stanza by John Keble:

> *Thou who hast given me eyes to see*
> *And love this sight as fair,*
> *Give me a heart to find out Thee,*
> *And read Thee everywhere.*

Alas, Farndale faces another kind of writing on the wall: Ichabod, or 'the glory has departed'. Progress threatens to flood the valley in order to provide water for Hull.

Meantime the loveliness flows like a green river that surges to become a fern-floored skyline. And the River Dove flows, too, flanked by five miles of April daffodils,

> *Continuous as the stars that shine*
> *And twinkle on the milky way . . .*

BOLTON PRIORY, YORKSHIRE

Wordsworth's poem, The Force of Prayer, recounts a tradition that Bolton Priory was founded by a woman whose son perished while trying to cross the River Wharfe. Numbed by grief, the mother hid herself:

> *Long, long in darkness did she sit,*
> *And her first words were, 'Let there be*
> *In Bolton, on the field of Wharf,*
> *A stately Priory*

History shows that the Priory was built by Augustinian Canons, in 1154, on the site of a Saxon manor. Four centuries later the Priory was still incomplete; no doubt because the monks had been too busy tending their sheep. At the Reformation the monastic buildings had their roofs removed, and the stone went to the making of Bolton Hall, a seat of the Earl of Cumberland.

YORK MINSTER

Daniel Defoe believed that York Minster was '. . . the beautifullest church in Britain'. Certainly it is the largest. From east to west it measures five hundred and thirty feet; of the one hundred and thirteen windows, three are eighty feet high. Building began in 1220 and ended two centuries later. In 1829 parts of the roof and choir were destroyed when a madman, named Jonathan Martin, set fire to the Minster. The Archbishop of York, Primate of England, resides at his palace of Bishop-thorpe, a few miles beyond the city.

During the 1960s it was found that the massive central tower (a late addition) had strained the fabric of the Minster. A world-wide appeal was therefore launched. The work of strengthening the masonry and reinforcing the foundations will cost several million pounds, and may last throughout the 1970s. Meantime, despite an army of workmen within and without, the life of the Minster goes on.

BURTON AGNES HALL, YORKSHIRE

'It looks finely . . .'. So wrote Celia Fiennes when she first saw Burton
Agnes Hall three centuries ago. Built by an Elizabethan, Sir Henry
Griffith, the Hall lies only an hour's walk from the wild Yorkshire
coast, in a parish that was named after an heiress, Agnes de Albermarle,
who in 1176 witnessed a deed concerning land in the district. At that
time a Norman manor house occupied the site.

   The Hall is approached via a yew-flanked drive from a gatehouse
(1610) bearing the carved shield of King James the First. Two hundred
years ago the Hall passed to the Boynton family, who still reside here.
All around, for miles and miles, a deep country heightens the bird-song
that we call silence. They farm here, and they supply the farmers; and
that is all. Is there a healthier way of life, or one more necessary to
life itself?

RIBBLESDALE

The River Ribble rises among rocks beside the road to Horton, not far from a Roman track through Dentdale. Thereafter it waters a realm of small country towns (Settle, Giggleswick) and of fellside hamlets (Stainforth, Knight Stainforth). Three mountains pierce the clouds—Whernside, Ingleborough, Pen-y-Ghent—rising like beacons from an ocean of sheepwalks, drystone walls, and becks blithe as a lark.

The wind bloweth where it listeth; snow comes early, and is late to leave. Ribblesdale is a man's country. It is tall, stern, strong; and through it strides the Pennine Way, the longest footpath in Britain, spanning two hundred and fifty miles from Peakland to the Cheviots. Ribblesdale defies the planner and the developer. It remains, in Milton's phrase,

Invulnerable, impenitrably arm'd . . .

CHATSWORTH, DERBYSHIRE

Mary Queen of Scots was imprisoned in a great Derbyshire house, owned by Bess of Hardwick, whose grandson, the first Duke of Devonshire, demolished it in order to build the grandest private residence in Britain. The Painted Hall, sixty feet long, has work by Titian, Holbein, Van Dyck, Poussin, Reynolds. The mediaeval tapestries and manuscripts are worth several fortunes.

The gardens were designed after the English style, the French style, the Italian style; a fountain plays 260 feet into the air. Fallow deer dapple the park, fleet as the cadence of Debussy. When Pastor Moritz toured England in 1782 he reported that Peakland contained seven wonders. 'The last of the Seven Wonders', he wrote, 'is Chatsworth, a mansion at the foot of a snow-covered mountain.'

CONISTON WATER

Many people are amazed when they discover that some of the finest Lakeland scenery lies in Lancashire; notably Coniston Water, which is five miles long and 190 feet deep. John Ruskin spent the last twenty-nine years of his life at Brantwood, a house overlooking Coniston Water; and he chose to be buried in Coniston churchyard rather than at Westminster Abbey. The village museum contains his model of the neighbouring mountains and their geological strata. Nearby, at Sawrey, lived Mrs Heelis, a sheep farmer, better known as Beatrix Potter.

But the greatest of them all was Wordsworth, who attended Hawkshead Grammar School:

> *. . . oft before the hours of school*
> *I travelled round our little lake, five miles*
> *Of pleasant wandering.*

WASDALE HEAD, CUMBERLAND

Locked-in among fells, the hamlet of Wasdale listens night and day to the call of the curlew and a babble of becks. Its church (almost as small as Culbone's on Exmoor) is seventeen feet wide, and can hold about forty-five worshippers. Parts of the roof are only five feet from the ground. Very old men heard their fathers speak of the church when it was used as a shippon. The lake here is the deepest in England.

No grain grows in these parts—the land is too high, the climate too harsh—but Herdwicks graze nearly 2,000 feet above the plain. The rest is silence, and the echo of that silence as it was distilled by Wordsworth:

> *Ye Presences of Nature in the sky*
> *And on the earth! Ye visions of the hills!*
> *And Souls of lonely places!*

KESWICK, CUMBERLAND

Keswick was the Old English *cesewic* or cheese farm; a tribute to the pastures at the foot of the mountains. German miners came here centuries ago, and grew rich by manufacturing lead pencils. Smugglers acquired a more anonymous reputation, pack-horseing their wares over the mountains from Cockermouth and Maryport.

Keswick today is commercial, car-crammed, crowned with bungalows and boarding-houses; but at early morning or in midwinter its environs would still be recognised by Robert Southey, Poet Laureate, who lived with his family at Greta Bank, on a Civil List pension of three pounds weekly. 'To think how many mouths', he sighed, 'I must feed out of one inkstand.' He was buried at Crosthwaite, a mile beyond the town, under a tombstone which the Portuguese provided in recognition of his interest in their kingdom.

The Publishers wish to thank the following for permission to reproduce photographs appearing in this book:

Hallam Ashley, for pages 117 and 145-9; Barnaby's Picture Library, for page 173; G. Douglas Bolton, for page 85; British Travel Association, for page 131; J. Allan Cash, for pages 81, 97, 109, 135 and 159; Eagle Photos Ltd, for page 115; John Etches of Bournemouth Ltd, for page 91; Noel Habgood, for pages 59, 61, 87, 101, 107, 141, 143, 171 and 175; A. F. Kersting, for pages 43, 47, 51, 57, 63, 65, 69-73, 75, 83, 93, 105, 113, 119, 123, 137, 139, 151, 155, 157, 161-5 and 169; Frank H. Meads, for page 125; Kenneth Scowen, for pages 17-41, 45, 49, 53, 55, 77, 79, 89, 95, 103, 111, 129, 133 and 167; Sound Stills Ltd, for page 67; Studio St Ives Ltd, for page 99; John Tarlton, for page 121; A. C. K. Ware Ltd, for page 153.